A Christmas Carol

The Ultimate Audio Revision Guide
By
Emily Bird
and
Jeff Thomas

Explore the religious elements of Scrooge's transformation from 'sinner' to 'second father'?

Introduction

- Although 'A Christmas Carol' tends towards a secular perspective, Scrooge's transformation is also framed in terms of a religious experience. Make an overarching statement about the extent to which you believe Scrooge's transformation to be a religious/secular.

Religion in 'A Christmas Carol'

1. In the initial description of Scrooge, he is described as a 'covetous old sinner!'. This tells the reader that his bad behaviour defies the teachings of Christianity.
2. The portly gentlemen are collecting in the name of Christian charity, Scrooge withholds funds at the start of the novella, but gives freely at the end. This suggests he has developed a Christian attitude towards the poor.
3. Marley's Ghost refers to the 'Christian spirit'.
4. The Ghost of Christmas Past emits a light and he could be considered symbolic of Jesus as he helps Scrooge to see the light and become a better person.
5. The Ghost of Christmas Yet To Come takes Scrooge to see his own gravestone, thereby reminding him that religion is an inseparable part of Victorian culture.
6. The good characters, such as Fred and Bob, often use religious language to express themselves and greet others.

Conclusion

- Sum up how much you believe Scrooge's journey to be religious, and how much of it is secular.

<u>Corresponding Key Quotes</u>

Religion in 'A Christmas Carol'

1. Stave 1 "A squeezing, wrenching, grasping, scraping, clutching, covetous old sinner!"
2. Stave 1 "Under the impression that they scarcely furnish Christian cheer of mind or body… a few of us are endeavouring to raise a fund to buy the poor some meat and drink, and means of warmth."
3. Stave 1 "Not to know that any Christian spirit working kindly in its little sphere, whatever it may be, will find its mortal life too short for its vast means of usefulness!"
4. Stave 2 "But the strangest thing about it was that from the crown of its head there sprung a bright clear jet of light"
   The Bible, John 8:12 "I am the light of the world. Whoever follows Me will never walk in the darkness, but will have the light of life."
5. Stave 4 "Scrooge crept towards it, trembling as he went; and, following the finger, read upon the stone of the neglected grave his own name, EBENEZER SCROOGE."
6. Stave 1 "A Merry Christmas, Uncle! God save you!" (Fred)
   Stave 3 "A Merry Christmas to us all, my dears. God bless us!" (Bob)

Key vocabulary for Scrooge

accepting, avaricious, Christian, contrite, converted, covetous, cruel, greedy, hard, mean, misanthropist, miserly, penitent, reborn, regretful, remorseful, repentant, rude, rueful, saved, sceptical, secular, sinner, skin-flint, transformed, usurer, worldly

What methods does The Ghost of Christmas Past use to reform Scrooge?

Introduction

♦ Consider the different methods used, including:

Upsetting Sights

1. Scrooge as a lonely schoolboy.
2. Scrooge with his sister when she was still alive.
3. Scrooge and his sister talking about their strict father.
4. Scrooge allowing Belle to break off their engagement.
5. Belle with her new devoted husband and loving family.

Role Models

1. Mr Fezziwig is both a businessman and a generous person.

Direct Contact with Scrooge

1. Chastises Scrooge over the issue of wearing its cap.
2. Challenges Scrooge when he displays emotion.
3. Reverse psychology when talking about Fezziwig.
4. Ignores Scrooge's protestations.
5. Reminds Scrooge he's only showing him the past, he's not making anything up.

Conclusion

♦ Sum up your discussion, and state which method you believe was most effective at helping Scrooge to better himself.

Corresponding Key Quotes

Upsetting Sights

1. Stave 2 "A solitary child, neglected by his friends."
2. Stave 2 "I have come to bring you home, dear brother!"
3. Stave 2 "Father is so much kinder than he used to be,"
4. Stave 2 "you will dismiss the recollection of it, gladly, as an unprofitable dream,"
5. Stave 2 "might have called him Father, and been a spring-time in the haggard winter of his life"

Role Models

1. Stave 2 "The happiness he gives is quite as great as if it cost a fortune."

Direct Contact With Scrooge

1. Stave 2 "What!... Would you so soon put out, with worldly hands, the light I give?"
2. Stave 2 "Your lip is trembling... And what is that upon your cheek?"
3. Stave 2 " He has spent but a few pounds... Is that so much that he deserves this praise?"
4. Stave 2 "the relentless Ghost pinioned him in both his arms, and forced him to observe what happened next"
5. Stave 2 "they are what they are, do not blame me!"

Key vocabulary for The Ghost of Christmas Past

challenging, eerie, ethereal, fair, firm, fluctuating, gentle, glowing, illuminating, incandescent, luminous, mild, mutable, otherworldly, relentless, stern, strange, unearthly

Is The Ghost of Christmas Present defined purely by his generous nature?

Introduction

- State how important the characteristic of generosity is in defining the Ghost of Christmas Present.
- Compare his generosity with his other qualities.

Generosity

1. The scene where he is introduced to the reader is filled with lavish descriptions of food, this shows off his generous nature and links him to the theme of Christmas and celebration.
2. His generosity to the poor highlights the theme of charity.
3. His good will is an example to Scrooge.
4. He allows Scrooge to stay and watch Fred's party.

Other Qualities

1. He is <u>perceptive</u>, for example, he points out that it is Man, not supernatural entities, who has imposed the 'no work on Sundays' rule.
2. He is <u>thorough</u>, he shows Scrooge lots of different locations where people are enjoying Christmas.
3. He can be <u>stern</u>, for example, he reflects Scrooge's heartless attitudes about workhouses back at Scrooge.

Conclusion

- Draw your points together showing to what extent you believe The Ghost of Christmas Present is defined by his generous nature, taking into account his other qualities.

Corresponding Key Quotes

Generosity

1. Stave 3 "Heaped up on the floor, to form a kind of throne, were turkeys, geese, game, poultry, brawn, great joints of meat, sucking-pigs, long wreaths of sausages, mince pies..."
2. Stave 3 "it was his own kind, generous, hearty nature, and his sympathy with all poor men,'
3. Stave 3 "outpouring, with a generous hand, its bright and harmless mirth on everything within its reach!"
4. Stave 3 "The Ghost was greatly pleased to find him in this mood, and looked upon him with such favour" The ghost says this can't be done, but lets him stay anyway!

Other Qualities

1. Stave 3 "There are some upon this earth of yours... who lay claim to know us, and who do their deeds of passion, pride, ill will, hatred, envy, bigotry and selfishness in our name, who are strange to us, and all our kith and kin, as if they had never lived. Remember that, and charge their doings on themselves, not us."
2. Stave 3 "A light shone from the window of a hut, and swiftly they advanced towards it. Passing through the wall of mud and stone, they found a cheerful company assembled round a glowing fire."
3. Stave 3 "'Are there no prisons?' said the Spirit, turning on him for the last time with his own words. 'Are there no workhouses?'"

Key vocabulary for The Ghost of Christmas Present

benevolent, bountiful, charitable, compassionate, empathetic, generous, insightful, jovial, magnanimous, observant, perceptive, stern, strict

Is The Ghost of Christmas Yet To Come more intimidating than Marley's Ghost?

Introduction

- Decide which spirit you think is the most intimidating and make a statement showing your thoughts.
- Use the following points to help you get started then add further opinions of your own.

Ghost of Christmas Yet To Come

1. This spirit resembles the Grim Reaper, so it has connotations of death.
2. It won't talk to Scrooge, it merely points things out.
3. Scrooge says he fears this ghost the most.
4. It tries to make Scrooge look at his own dead body.
5. It shows Scrooge his own grave.

Marley's Ghost

1. Marley's Ghost is the first to appear, and its unexpected arrival is unnerving.
2. Marley's Ghost is a direct representation of what Scrooge will become if he doesn't change his miserly ways.
3. Marley's Ghost exists in a torturous state.
4. Scrooge is at times both dismissive and terrified by this ghost.

Conclusion

- Make a summative statement regarding which spirit you believe to be the most intimidating.

Corresponding Key Quotes

The Ghost of Christmas Yet To Come

1. Stave 4 "It was shrouded in a deep black garment, which concealed its head, its face, its form"
2. Stave 4 "The Spirit answered not, but pointed onwards with its hand."
3. Stave 4 "'Ghost of the Future!' he exclaimed. 'I fear you more than any spectre I have seen.'"
4. Stave 4 "Still the Ghost pointed with an unmoved finger to the head."
5. Stave 4 "Scrooge crept towards it, trembling as he went' and, following the finger, read upon the stone of the neglected grave his own name, EBENEZER SCROOGE."

Marley's Ghost

1. Stave 1 "without a pause, it came on through the heavy door, and passed into the room before his eyes."
2. Stave 1 "the weight and length of the strong coil you bear... was full as heavy and as long as this, seven Christmas Eves ago. You have laboured on it since."
3. Stave 1 "No rest, no peace. Incessant torture of remorse."
4. Stave 1 "You may be an undigested bit of beef, a blot of mustard" "the spectre's voice disturbed the very marrow in his bones."

Key vocabulary for The Phantom

compassionate, determined, discomforting, disturbing, eerie, enigmatic, ethereal, gloomy, grand, inscrutable, intimidating, methodical, mysterious, persistent, stately, steely, sympathetic, systematic, thorough, unnerving, unsettling, unwavering, wraithlike

Why is Fred such an important supporting character in 'A Christmas Carol'?

Introduction

- Briefly outline why Fred is such a key supporting character.

Fred

1. Fred expresses ideas about Christmas and about the nature of love, and in doing so, he is a <u>role model</u> for Scrooge and reader alike.

2. Fred is not daunted by Scrooge's bad behaviour and perseveres in trying to convert his uncle to a happier person. His sympathy for Scrooge is <u>symbolic of the spirit of good will</u>.

3. Fred tells his wife and guests that he pities Scrooge; he feels compassion rather than negative feelings towards his rude uncle, in this, Fred continues to be the <u>epitome of goodness</u>.

4. Fred gives his condolences to Bob Cratchit on hearing of the death of Tiny Tim, and tells Bob that he can rely on him for any help necessary, here Fred is the <u>embodiment of empathy and charity</u>, which is a key theme in the novella.

5. Fred welcomes his uncle with open arms when Scrooge does decide to take up the invitation to Christmas lunch, showing that he forgives Scrooge all previous bad behaviour. Here Fred is the very <u>ideal of clemency</u>.

6. Fred is jovial and generous in the extreme, like <u>a mortal version of the Ghost of Christmas Present</u>, showing that being pure and kind is not just the preserve of the ghosts.

7. Fred is a <u>counterpoint to Scrooge</u>, proving that rudeness is not endemic within the family.

Conclusion

- Sum up your opinions about Fred.

Corresponding Key Quotes

Fred

1. Stave 1 "I have always though of Christmas-time… as a good time: a kind, forgiving, charitable, pleasant time"
2. Stave 3 "I mean to give him the same chance every year, whether he likes it or not"
3. Stave 3 "I am sorry for him; I couldn't be angry with him if I tried. Who suffers by his ill whims? Himself, always"
4. Stave 4 "'Heartily sorry', he said, 'for your good wife. If I can be of service to you in any way,' he said, giving me his card, 'that's where I live. Pray come to me.'"
5. Stave 5 "Let him in! It is a mercy he didn't shake his arm off. He was at home in five minutes. Nothing could be heartier."
6. Stave 3 "If you should happen, by any unlikely chance, to know a man more blessed in a laugh that Scrooge's nephew, all I can say is, I should like to know him too."
7. Stave 1 "'Come, then,' returned the nephew gaily. 'What right have you to be dismal? What reason have you to be morose? You're rich enough.'"

Key vocabulary for Fred

attentive, benevolent, breezy, caring, cheerful, compassionate, considerate, determined, empathetic, forgiving, generous, gentle, good-natured, joyful, jovial, kind, magnanimous, merry, noble, persistent, sympathetic, tenacious, thoughtful, understanding, warm-hearted

How does Dickens use language to make the ghosts distinctive?

Introduction

- State your opinion on how Dickens makes the ghosts unique.

Ghost of Christmas Past

1. This ghost is characterised in terms of vulnerability, it's at once both a child and an old man.
2. This ghost is dressed in a white robe to emphasize that it's helping Scrooge to wipe the slate clean and start anew.
3. This ghost is characterised by imagery to do with light, as it's illuminating Scrooge's path to redemption.

Ghost of Christmas Present

1. This ghost is characterised in terms of generosity.
2. This ghost is dressed in a green robe to align it with Victorian images of Father Christmas, this emphasizes that it's helping Scrooge to get in touch with the celebratory nature of life.
3. This ghost is characterised by sensory language and is often surrounding by luscious sights, tastes and feelings.

Ghost of Christmas Yet To Come

1. This ghost is characterised in terms of terror.
2. This ghost is reminiscent of the Grim Reaper to remind Scrooge that death and then eternal torment await if he doesn't change his ways.
3. This ghost is characterised by figurative language connected with darkness and foreboding to represent the fact that the future can be a source of anxiety.

Corresponding Key Quotes

Ghost of Christmas Past

1. Stave 2 "like a child: yet not so like a child as like an old man".
2. Stave 2 "It wore a tunic of purest white"
3. Stave 2 "its light was burning high and bright; and dimly connecting that with its influence over him".

Ghost of Christmas Present

1. Stave 3 "it was his own kind, generous, hearty nature, and his sympathy with all poor men".
2. Stave 3 "it was clothed in one simple deep green robe, or mantle, bordered with white fur".
3. Stave 3 "Heaped up on the floor, to form a kind of throne, were turkeys, geese, game, poultry, brawn, great joins of meat, sucking-pigs, long wreaths of sausages, mince pies".

Ghost of Christmas Yet To Come

1. Stave 4 "its mysterious presence filled him with a solemn dread".
2. Stave 4 "Still the ghost pointed downwards to the grave by which it stood".
3. Stave 4 "But if the course be departed from, the ends will change. Say it is thus with what you show me!".

Key vocabulary for the language

detail, didactic, dual purpose, educational, entertaining, figurative language, humour, informative, instructive, lists, moralizing, moving, omniscient narrator, paradoxes, pathetic fallacy, perplexing imagery, personification, playful, puzzles, similes

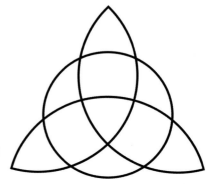

How does the structure add tension to 'A Christmas Carol'?

Introduction

- Make an opening statement about how Dickens uses the structure to create tension. Use the points below and your own ideas.

Tiny Tim

1. In Stave 3 The Ghost of Christmas Present says Tiny Tim might die, and in Stave 4 The Ghost of Christmas Yet to Come confirms this.
2. The narrator keeps the reader guessing right until the penultimate paragraph before revealing the happy news.

Fred's invitation to Scrooge

1. In Stave 1, Fred invites Scrooge to come to Christmas lunch.
2. Scrooge rudely rejects this offer.
3. In Stave 5, Scrooge now wants to join in with his family's celebrations but worries that they won't accept him.
4. Fred and his wife do accept Scrooge in keeping with the spirit of Christmas.

Scrooge's reaction to the ghosts

1. Initially Scrooge scoffs at Marley's Ghost, and it seems doubtful if he is able to accept any supernatural help.
2. He extinguishes The Ghost of Christmas Past, jeopardising his chance for further visitations.
3. But, by the time The Ghost of Christmas Future arrives, Scrooge has become fully receptive to spiritual assistance.

Corresponding Key Quotes

Tiny Tim

1. Stave 3 "I see a vacant seat… If these shadow remain unaltered by the Future, the child will die."
2. Stave 5 "and to Tiny Tim, who did *not* die, he was a second father".

Fred's Invitation to Scrooge

1. Stave 1 "Uncle. Come! Dine with us tomorrow".
2. Stave 1 "Scrooge said that he would see him ——. Yes, indeed he did. He went the whole length of the expression, and said that he would see him in that extremity first".
3. Stave 5 "He passed the door a dozen times before he had the courage to go up and knock".
4. Stave 5 "'Will you let me in, Fred?' Let him in! It is a mercy he didn't shake his arm off. He was at home in five minutes".

Scrooge's reaction to the ghosts

1. Stave 1 "There's more of gravy than of grave about you, whatever you are!".
2. Stave 2 "he seized the extinguisher cap, and by a sudden action pressed it down upon its head".
3. Stave 4 "I am prepared to bear your company, and do it with a thankful heart".

Key vocabulary for the structure

apex, cause and effect, chronological, climax, closure, conclusion, consequence, crisis, culmination, denouement, development, exposition, final, finale, gathering, impending, introduction, novella, opening, pace, penultimate, progressive, revelation, sections, sequential

How is the theme of family used in 'A Christmas Carol'?

Introduction

- State which aspects of the family theme you find interesting.

Scrooge's Family

1. Dickens hints that at times, Scrooge's father was strict, which helps to explain why Scrooge becomes so harsh.
2. Scrooge's mother is not mentioned, suggesting that Scrooge grew up without a maternal figure.
3. Scrooge's sister is loving and caring, but dies young, so Scrooge has no sympathetic family members (until Fred grows up), suggesting Scrooge may have been lonely.
4. Fred is a loving and affectionate nephew, willing to overlook Scrooge's mean personality and rude behaviour.
5. The fact that nobody attends Scrooge's deathbed suggests that he becomes increasingly hostile to Fred and would have driven even him away, if he hadn't changed.

The Cratchit Family

1. The Cratchit family are caring towards each other and provide an example of how love is more important than being rich.
2. Tiny Tim instils new feelings of responsibility and affection in Scrooge, thus helping Scrooge to reform his bad character.

Belle's Family

1. Scrooge witnesses Belle, happy with her family, and realises that he could have had this life.

Corresponding Key Quotes

Scrooge's Family

1. Stave 2 "Father is so much kinder than he used to be'
2. There is no mention of Scrooge's mother in the novella.
3. Stave 2 "Always a delicate creature, whom a breath might have withered... She died a woman,"
4. Stave 1 "'Don't be angry, Uncle. Come! Dine with us tomorrow"
5. Stave 4 "He lay, in the dark, empty house, with not a man, a woman or a child to say that he was kind to me in this or that"

The Cratchit Family

1. Stave 3 "Then all the Cratchit family drew round the hearth in what Bob Cratchit called a circle... and at Bob Cratchit's elbow stood the family display of glass. Two tumblers and a custard cup without a handle"
2. Stave 3 "'Spirit', said Scrooge with an interest he had never felt before, 'tell me if Tiny Tim will live'"

Belle's Family

1. Stave 2 "when he thought that such another creature, quite as graceful and as full of promise, might have called him Father...his sight grew very dim indeed"

Key vocabulary for the theme of family

affectionate, caring, celebration, children, devotion, generations, harsh, humility, isolated, joy, life, lonely, loving, motherless, rejected, responsible, sequestered, tender, warm

What does A Christmas Carol teach the reader about Victorian Businesses?

Introduction

- Introduce the idea that A Christmas Carol teaches the reader about a variety of business establishments including food shops, pawn-brokers and financial services.

Food Shops

1. All the food shops in A Christmas Carol are portrayed as places that exude a sense of plenty, and this is in keeping with the festive spirit of the novel. The produce on offer in the food shops is wide ranging and exotic; this reflects the fact that Victorian London was at the centre of the British Empire and traded with many countries around the world.

Pawnbrokers

1. Joe, who runs the pawnbrokers is happy to accept goods that he knows are stolen. This reflects the fact that there were illegal businesses operating in Victorian London.

Office Business

1. Scrooge is a money-lender by trade and is ruthless in his pursuit of clients who default on repayments. He represents all Victorian businessmen who were greedy and immoral.
2. Fezziwig also runs an office, but he is depicted as a kind and generous employer, and is the antithesis of Scrooge.

Conclusion

- Make a final statement which draws together your observations about Victorian businesses.

Corresponding Key Quotes

Food Shops

1. Stave 3 "blended scents of tea and coffee... the raisins were so plentiful and rare, the almonds so extremely white, the sticks of cinnamon, so long and straight, the other spices so delicious... the figs were moist and pulpy... the French plums blushed in modest tartness".

Pawnbrokers

1. Stave 4 "'You don't mean to say you took 'em down, rings and all, with him lying there?' said Joe. 'Yes, I do' replied the woman... old Joe, producing a flannel bag with money in it, told out their several gains upon the ground."

Office Business

1. Stave 4 "before that time, we shall be ready with the money; and even though we were not, it would be bad fortune indeed to find so merciless a creditor in his successor.

2. Stave 2 "Mr and Mrs Fezziwig took their stations, one on either side the door, and, shaking hands with every person individually as he or she went out, wished him or her a Merry Christmas."

Key vocabulary for the historical context

1834 Poor Law, benefactors, bounty, British Empire, Cornucopia, excess, exotic produce, illicit trade, Industrial Revolution, malefactors, Panopticon prison, pawnbrokers, plenty, The Crank-handle, The Separate System, The Treadmill, Union Workhouses, worldwide trade

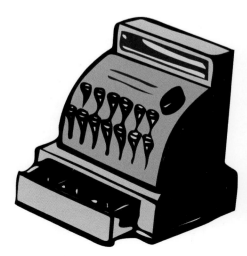

About us

Jeff Thomas

Until recently, Jeff worked as a history teacher, specialising in alternative teaching methods. Jeff has also worked alongside the University of Sussex in the role of PGCE mentor, and has trained numerous student teachers. With the ever growing success of Revision Rocks, Jeff has now stopped teaching, in order to work full-time on developing new and exciting revision aids. Jeff also works as an expert examiner for Edexcel.

Jeff has appeared on: BBC 5 live, BBC Sussex, Kent, London and Surrey to talk about cutting edge revision techniques and Revision Rocks. Jeff has also been featured in the Times Educational Supplement (TES) on two occasions, in relation to revising through song. Jeff has also made many radio appearances for the BBC to discuss issues relating to history and secondary education, which he says makes him feel very important within the world of history teaching.

Emily Bird

Emily trained as an English teacher, but has also taught other subjects including: History, Psychology and R.E. Emily developed her teaching career in the area of SEN, and has a great deal of experience in working with dyslexic and autistic pupils. Emily worked with the University of Brighton as a Professional Tutor and mentor to trainee teachers. Over the years, Emily has been a regular examiner for AQA. Emily now works full time on writing material and adding to the Revision Rocks range.

Customer satisfaction guaranteed: We want you to be entirely happy with our products. If for any reason there is a problem, please contact us directly: jeff.thomas@revisionrocks.co.uk and we promise to solve the issue.